This Book Belongs To:

_____

COPYRIGHT © 2004 Nanci Bell
Gander Publishing
450 Front Street
Avila Beach, CA 93424
805-541-5523 • 800-554-1819

VISUALIZING AND VERBALIZING AND V/V ARE REGISTERED TRADEMARKS OF NANCI BELL.

All rights reserved. No part of this material shall be reproduced or transmitted in any form or by any means, electronic or mechanical, including photocopying, recording, or by any information or retrieval system, without prior written permission from the Publisher. Printed in the U.S.A.

14  13  12  11       4  6  7  8

ISBN 0-945856-48-2     978-0-945856-48-1

# Overview and Directions

This workbook is offered to provide a wider selection of material for practice developing gestalt imagery and language comprehension with the *Visualizing and Verbalizing for Language Comprehension and Thinking*® (V/V®) program.

Following the steps of V/V®, detail and gestalt imagery are developed with Sentence by Sentence, Multiple Sentence, Whole Paragraph, and Paragraph by Paragraph V/V® stimulation.

The V/V® workbooks contain high-imagery stories and the following workbook activities:

- Imagery questions
- Picture summary exercises
- Word summary prompts
- Page summary prompts
- Main idea exercises
- Higher order thinking (HOT) questions
- Paragraph writing prompts

Before the student begins each story, he/she should decode each vocabulary word and visualize the meaning. This will help create imagery and develop contextual fluency. When answering imagery questions, the student may write phrases or partial sentences to describe his/her imagery.

These workbooks have been written specifically to help students learn and discover the wonder of the written word by improving gestalt imagery, critical thinking, and writing skills. Once these skills are developed, the possibilities are endless.

Remember, you can help students do this. You can do anything!

Nanci Bell
2004

---

**There are three workbooks at each reading level:**

**Book A • Sentence by Sentence**

**Book B • Sentence by Sentence and Multiple Sentence**

**Book C • Multiple Sentence, Whole Paragraph, and Paragraph by Paragraph**

# Meet Ivan!

I am Ivan, King of the Neighborhood. I'm big and wide and full of pride!

I **love** to sleep!

I am a cat!

# 1 Fire!

When the loud bell rang at the fire station, the men jumped to their feet. They put on yellow suits, helmets, and boots. Then they ran to their truck and raced down the streets with the siren on. They stopped at a big fire, jumped off the truck, and pulled out their hoses.

**Sentence by Sentence**
Date: _____

**Vocabulary to Visualize:**

**station:** the main office of the police or fire department
**helmet:** a hard hat worn to protect the head
**race:** goes very fast
**siren:** a signal with a loud sound that warns people

## A  Picture This: When the loud bell rang at the fire station, the men jumped to their feet.

*Which best matches your picture?*  ○   ○

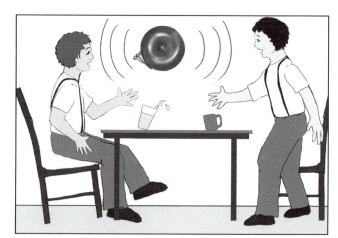

Underline the answer that best matches your own picture.

| | | | |
|---|---|---|---|
| **1.** How many men did you see? | one | none | some |
| **2.** What did you see them wearing? | pants and shirts | swimsuits | shorts and hats |
| **3.** How loud was the bell you heard? | like a whisper | like a nearby plane | |
| **4.** Where did you see the men? | at the beach | in a room | on a truck |

**Did you picture all of the structure words?** Check each one you saw in your image.
☐ What   ☐ Size   ☐ Color   ☐ Number   ☐ Shape   ☐ Where
☐ Movement   ☐ Mood   ☐ Background   ☐ Perspective   ☐ When   ☐ Sound

**B** **Picture This:** They put on yellow suits, helmets, and boots.

| | | | |
|---|---|---|---|
| 1. What did those words make you picture? | men dressing | men sleeping | men laughing |
| 2. How did you see the men moving? | fast | slow | |
| 3. What did you see them putting on first? | _____ | | |
| 4. What did you picture for their helmets? | soft hoods | hard hats | hard masks |
| 5. How did you picture their boots? | thick and heavy | thin and furry | pretty and sparkly |
| 6. What color did you picture their suits? | _____ | | |
| 7. What did you see for their suits? | fuzzy jacket and pants | rubbery jacket and pants | |

**C** **Picture This:** Then they ran to their truck and raced down the streets with the siren on.

| | | |
|---|---|---|
| 1. What did those words make you picture? | men sitting on a stopped truck | men sitting on a speeding truck |
| 2. What did you see for them running? | legs moving fast     legs still | legs moving slow |
| 3. What did you see for their truck? | a big truck with ladders | a small truck with hay in it |
| 4. How did you see them racing with the siren on? | men running in the street | men on a fast-moving truck |
| 5. Where did you see the streets? | in a city     in a neighborhood | at a beach |
| 6. What did you hear for the siren in your picture? | a long, loud sound | short, soft beeps |

**D** **Picture This:** They stopped at a big fire, jumped off the truck, and pulled out their hoses.

*Which best matches your picture?*

Underline the answer that best matches your own picture.

1. What did you see for the fire?          a campfire          a fireplace          a burning building
2. How did you see the truck stopping?          suddenly          slowly          not at all
3. How did you see the men jumping?          down from truck to ground          up from ground to truck
4. What did you see for their hoses?          thick, long tubes with metal ends          thin, cloth tubes with strings

**Picture Summary:**
Number your images in order.

___ The men leaped off of the truck and pulled out hoses.

___ The men jumped up at the sound of the bell ringing.

___ The firetruck raced through the streets with the men holding onto it.

___ The men dressed in yellow suits, boots, and helmets as quickly as they could.

**Word Summary:**
Fill in the blanks using the words listed below.

The bell _____ and the men jumped up.

They put on yellow boots and _____.

Then they ran to the fire _____, and rode it as it sped down the streets. At a big fire, they jumped off and pulled out their _____.

**truck          helmets          hoses          rang**

**Main Idea:**

Connect these with a line.

Firemen put on yellow suits and helmets.

Firemen got ready to make a fire.

Firemen got ready to fight a fire.

a detail

main idea

wrong

**Vocabulary Check:**

Draw a line from the word to its meaning.

station

siren

hose

race

helmet

a loud sound that warns people

goes very fast

the main office of a police or fire department

a tube that liquid can flow through

a hard hat worn to protect the head

**HOT Questions:**

1. Why do you think the loud bell is important? _____

_____

2. Why do you think the firemen dressed in suits, helmets, and boots? _____

_____

3. What do you think would have happened if the truck was not fast? _____

_____

4. What do you think happened next? _____

_____

# 2 Starfish

The spiny-skinned starfish lives on the sea floor. She creeps across the sand with her five strong arms. When she bumps a clam, she pulls it open. After lunch, she leaves the empty shell and searches for more.

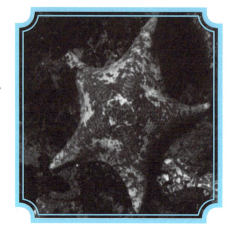

**Sentence by Sentence**
Date: _____

**Vocabulary to Visualize:**
**spiny:** spiky
**starfish:** a sea animal with five or more arms shaped like a star
**creep:** move slowly close to the ground
**clam:** a soft-bodied sea animal that lives in a two-part shell

## A Picture This: The spiny-skinned starfish lives on the sea floor.

*Which best matches your picture?*  ○  ○

**Underline or write in the answer that best matches your own picture.**

1. What color did you picture the starfish? _____
2. How did you picture her skin?            rough and bumpy            smooth and slick
3. What size starfish did you picture?      big as a man's hand        big as a merry-go-round
4. Where did you see her living?            bottom of the sea          on the waves

---
**Did you picture all of the structure words? Check each one you saw in your image.**
☐ What     ☐ Size     ☐ Color       ☐ Number      ☐ Shape    ☐ Where
☐ Movement ☐ Mood     ☐ Background  ☐ Perspective ☐ When     ☐ Sound

**B** **Picture This:** She creeps across the sand with her five strong arms.

1. What did those words make you picture?   starfish walking   starfish crawling   starfish swimming
2. How did you see her creeping?   crawling with all five arms   walking on two legs
3. How fast did you see her creeping?   slow like a snail   fast like a bunny
4. How did you see that her arms were strong?   skinny arms   fat, floppy arms   thick, tough arms
5. How many arms did you see? _____
6. What did you picture for the sand?   wet, smooth, and flat   big, dry dunes   hard and bumpy

**C** **Picture This:** When she bumps a clam, she pulls it open.

1. What did those words make you picture?   starfish with a ball   starfish with a clamshell
2. What color did you picture the clam? _____
3. How did you see the starfish bump the clam?   she nudged in   she flicked it away
4. What did you see her pulling on?   a solid rock   the clam's two shells
5. What did you see her pulling with?   her arms   her teeth
6. How did you see that the clam was open?   shells apart   shells together

**Picture This:** After lunch, she leaves the empty shell and searches for more.

*Which best matches your picture?*

○   ○

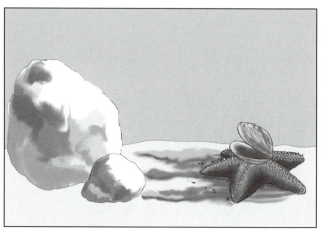

**Underline the answer that best matches your own picture.**

1. What did you see the starfish eat?           a sandwich        a mouse        a clam
2. How did you see her searching for more?    taking a nap    crawling away    eating the shell
3. What did you see for her mood?            still hungry        full        sleepy
4. How did you see that the shell was empty?    water inside    clam inside    crab inside

**Picture Summary:**

Number your images in order.

- The starfish ran into a clam and pulled its shell open.
- The starfish moved slowly across the sand, crawling with its five arms.
- The starfish left the empty shell of the clam and went searching for more.
- The starfish lived at the bottom of the sea on the sand.

**Word Summary:**

Fill in the blanks using the words listed below.

The spiny-skinned starfish _____ slowly across the sea floor. She _____ into a clam, and then pulled it open with her _____ strong arms. After lunch, she left the _____ shell and searched for more clams.

**moved        empty        bumped        five**

**Main Idea:**

Connect these with a line.

A starfish found and ate a fish.

A starfish found and ate a clam.

A starfish has spiny skin.

a detail

main idea

wrong

**Vocabulary Check:**

Draw a line from the word to its meaning.

starfish — spiky

creep — the ocean

spiny — a sea animal that lives in a two-part shell

sea — move slowly and close to the ground

clam — a sea animal with five or more arms

**HOT Questions:**

1. Why do you think the starfish creeps around instead of sitting in one place? _____

2. Why do you think she needs strong arms? _____

3. Where do you think the empty shells came from? _____

4. Why do you think she goes looking for more? _____

# 3 Frog Meal

Sentence by Sentence
Date: _____

The green frog sits quietly on the leafy branch. With his bulging eyes, he spots a tiny fly as it buzzes nearby. He slowly opens his mouth and then snaps out his long, sticky tongue. Lunch!

**Vocabulary to Visualize:**

**bulging:** curving or sticking out
**buzz:** a low humming sound
**snap:** to move so fast it makes a sharp noise

## A  Picture This: The green frog sits quietly on the leafy branch.

*Which best matches your picture?*  ○   ○

**Underline the answer that best matches your own picture.**

| | | | |
|---|---|---|---|
| **1.** How big did you picture the frog? | big as a mouse | big as a baby | big as a fly |
| **2.** How did you picture his skin? | rough | scaly | smooth |
| **3.** What did you see him doing? | creeping | not moving | jumping |
| **4.** Where did you see him sitting? | on the ground | in the grass | in a tree |

**Did you picture all of the structure words? Check each one you saw in your image.**
☐ What    ☐ Size    ☐ Color    ☐ Number    ☐ Shape    ☐ Where
☐ Movement    ☐ Mood    ☐ Background    ☐ Perspective    ☐ When    ☐ Sound

**B** **Picture This:** With his bulging eyes, he spots a tiny fly as it buzzes nearby.

| | | | |
|---|---|---|---|
| 1. | What did those words make you picture? | frog seeing a bug | frog seeing a bird |
| 2. | How did you see the frog spot the fly? | his ears wiggle | his eyes move |
| 3. | How big was the fly you pictured? | big as a bee | big as a house |
| 4. | Where did you see the fly buzzing? | close to the frog | far away from the frog |
| 5. | How did you see that the fly was buzzing? | wings flapping | wings folded |

**C** **Picture This:** He slowly opens his mouth and then snaps out his long, sticky tongue.

| | | | | |
|---|---|---|---|---|
| 1. | What did those words make you picture? | frog with tongue out | frog with mouth closed | |
| 2. | How did you see his mouth opening? | lips closing | lips coming apart | |
| 3. | How did you see his tongue move? | slow | fast | |
| 4. | What color did you picture for his tongue? | _____ | | |
| 5. | How long did you picture his tongue? | long as a car | long as a mouse | long as a peanut |
| 6. | How did you see his tongue as sticky? | gluey | smooth | |

**Picture This:** Lunch!

*Which best matches your picture?*

○    ○

**Underline the answer that best matches your own picture.**

1. What did you see the frog eat?   a leaf   a fly   a sandwich
2. How did you see him eating?   he sucked his tongue in   he spit out
3. Where did you see the fly?   in the air   on the frog's tongue
4. When did you see this happen?   night   day

**Picture Summary:**

Number your images in order.

▢ The frog opened his mouth and shot out his tongue.

▢ The frog waited on the leafy branch.

▢ The frog spotted a tiny fly nearby in the sky with his big, bulging eyes.

▢ The frog ate his lunch.

**Word Summary:**

Fill in the blanks using the words listed below.

The green frog waited on the _____ of the tree. With his big eyes, he saw a _____ nearby. He slowly opened his _____ and then _____ his long, sticky tongue out. Then he ate lunch.

**snapped**   **fly**   **branch**   **mouth**

**Main Idea:**

Connect these with a line.

| | |
|---|---|
| The frog caught and ate a spider. | a detail |
| The frog sat on a branch. | main idea |
| The frog caught and ate a fly. | wrong |

**Vocabulary Check:**

Draw a line from the word to its meaning.

| | |
|---|---|
| bulging | part of a tree |
| frog | to move so fast it makes a sharp noise |
| snap | curving or sticking out |
| buzz | a small animal with a big mouth and long legs |
| branch | a low humming sound |

**HOT Questions:**

1. Why do you think the frog sits quietly? _____

2. Why do you think he opens his mouth slowly? _____

3. Why do you think he snaps out his tongue? _____

4. What do you think his "lunch" is? _____

# 4  The Long Jump

The crowd cheers as the woman sprints down the runway.  When she reaches the edge of a sandpit, she jumps.  She flies in the air and lands on her heels in the soft sand near the end of the pit.  The sandy woman gets up and smiles at the crowd, sure she has won.

**Sentence by Sentence**
Date: _____

**Vocabulary to Visualize:**

**sprint:** run a short distance very fast
**runway:** a long, straight track to run on
**sandpit:** a shallow hole filled with sand
**heel:** rounded back end of foot
**sandy:** covered with sand

## A  Picture This: The crowd cheers as the woman sprints down the runway.

*Which best matches your picture?*  ◯   ◯

**Underline or write in the answer that best matches your own picture.**

| | | |
|---|---|---|
| **1.** How old was the woman you pictured? | _____ years old | |
| **2.** What did you picture for how she ran? | very fast | very slow |
| **3.** How did you picture the runway? | a dirt track | a snowy trail |
| **4.** How did you picture the crowd? | lots of loud people | lots of silent people |

**Did you picture all of the structure words?  Check each one you saw in your image.**

| ☐ What | ☐ Size | ☐ Color | ☐ Number | ☐ Shape | ☐ Where |
|---|---|---|---|---|---|
| ☐ Movement | ☐ Mood | ☐ Background | ☐ Perspective | ☐ When | ☐ Sound |

## B

**Picture This:** When she reaches the edge of a sandpit, she jumps.

1. What did those words make you picture?   woman digging   woman leaping   woman walking
2. What did you see for the sandpit?   a hole in the ground with sand in it   a metal ring with water in it
3. What shape did you see for the sandpit?   circle   triangle   rectangle
4. What did you see for the edge of the sandpit?   the side of the pit   the middle of the pit
5. How did you picture the woman jumping?   low to the ground   high in the air
6. Where did you see her arms as she jumped?   crossed over her chest   reaching forward   straight down

## C

**Picture This:** She flies in the air and lands on her heels in the soft sand near the end of the pit.

1. What did those words make you picture?   woman hitting sand with heels   woman flying past sandpit
2. How did you see that she flies in the air?   she flaps her wings   she leaps far and high
3. How long did you see her jump taking?   seconds   hours   days
4. Where did you see her land?   in the sand   outside the pit   on the runway
5. How did you picture her landing?   on her head   on her heels   on her knees
6. What did you see the sand doing when she landed in it?   it cracked   it squished

# D

**Picture This:** The sandy woman gets up and smiles at the crowd, sure she has won.

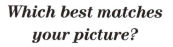

*Which best matches your picture?*

**Underline the answer that best matches your own picture.**

1. How did you see the woman get up?           she stood quickly         she lay down
2. How did you see that she smiled at the crowd?        she frowned        she grinned
3. Where did you see her standing?          in front of the crowd       behind the crowd
4. How did you see that she was sandy?     she had sand all over her     she had no sand on her

## Picture Summary:
Number your images in order.

- The woman landed on her heels in the sand at the end of the pit.
- The woman got up and smiled at the people watching.
- The woman ran down the runway as the crowd cheered her on.
- The woman got to the edge of the sandpit and jumped high and far over the sand.

## Word Summary:
Fill in the blanks using the words listed below.

The woman _____ down the runway toward the sandpit as the _____ cheered. At the edge of the sand, she _____ and flew through the air. She landed on her _____ in the sand. She got up smiling, sure she had won.

**jumped        crowd        heels        sprinted**

**Main Idea:**
Connect these with a line.

| | |
|---|---|
| The woman landed on her heels. | a detail |
| The woman jumped down. | main idea |
| The woman jumped far. | wrong |

**Vocabulary Check:**
Draw a line from the word to its meaning.

| | |
|---|---|
| sandy | lots of people together |
| heel | run a short distance very fast |
| sandpit | a shallow hole filled with sand |
| crowd | covered with sand |
| sprint | rounded back end of foot |

**HOT Questions:**

1. Why do you think there was a crowd? _____

2. Why do you think the woman jumped into a pit of sand and not hard ground? _____

3. Why do you think she was sandy at the end of the story? _____

4. What do you think her mood would be if she landed in the middle of the pit? _____

## Wash Before You Eat

Sentence by Sentence
Date: _____

The hungry raccoon wades through the stream and climbs up on a rock. He paws at the water below. He finds a small frog on the stream bottom and snatches it up. Then he eats his tasty treat.

**Vocabulary to Visualize:**

**raccoon:** a furry brown and black animal
**wade:** walk through water or snow
**stream:** a small river
**paws:** feel for; grab at
**snatch:** take quickly
**treat:** food; a snack

### A  Picture This: The hungry raccoon wades through the stream and climbs up on a rock.

*Which best matches your picture?*  ○   ○

**Underline or write in the answer that best matches your own picture.**

| | | | |
|---|---|---|---|
| **1.** What size was the raccoon you pictured? | like a cat | like a horse | like a frog |
| **2.** What color did you picture for his fur? | | | |
| **3.** Where did you see him wading? | in the ocean | in a small river | in a pond |
| **4.** Where did you see him after he waded through the stream? | | on a rock | on the shore |

**Did you picture all of the structure words?  Check each one you saw in your image.**

☐ What ☐ Size ☐ Color ☐ Number ☐ Shape ☐ Where
☐ Movement ☐ Mood ☐ Background ☐ Perspective ☐ When ☐ Sound

**Picture This:** He paws at the water below.

1. What did those words make you picture?     raccoon with paws in stream     raccoon with nose in stream
2. How did you see him pawing at the water?     touching the top of the water     reaching in the water
3. How deep in the water did you see his paws?     up to his wrists     up to his elbows     up to his shoulders
4. How did you picture the water feeling?     hot     warm     cold
5. How did you picture the water?     clear     dirty     muddy

**Picture This:** He finds a small frog on the stream bottom and snatches it up.

1. What did those words make you picture?     raccoon grabbing a fish     raccoon grabbing a frog
2. How did you see him finding something in the stream?     paws feeling around     looking with eyes
3. How did you picture the frog?     furry and brown     spiny and silver     shiny and green
4. How did you see the raccoon snatching the frog?     with one paw     with both paws
5. How did you see his face when he snatches?     smiling     crying     yelling
6. How did you see the frog in the raccoon's paws?     sitting still     flying away     fighting to get free

**Picture This:** Then he eats his tasty treat.

*Which best matches your picture?*  ○  ○

**Underline the answer that best matches your own picture.**

| | | | | |
|---|---|---|---|---|
| **1.** How did you see the raccoon eating? | sucking | | chewing | licking |
| **2.** What did you see him eating? | a frog | | a fish | a tiger |
| **3.** How did you picture his mouth? | no teeth | | lots of teeth | one tooth |
| **4.** What size did you picture the frog? | small as a cracker | | small as a marble | small as a dog |

**Picture Summary:**

Number your images in order.

▪ The raccoon ate his snack.

▪ The raccoon walked in the water of the stream and climbed a rock.

▪ The raccoon dipped his paws into the water and felt around.

▪ The raccoon found a small frog and snatched it up and out of the water.

**Word Summary:**

Fill in the blanks using the words listed below.

The raccoon _____ in the stream. He climbed up on a _____. Then the raccoon _____ the water. He grabbed a small frog on the stream bottom. He ate his _____.

**pawed**   **treat**   **waded**   **rock**

**Main Idea:**

Connect these with a line.

| A raccoon found and ate a leaf. | | a detail |
|---|---|---|
| A raccoon found and ate a frog. | | main idea |
| A raccoon put his paws in the water. | | wrong |

**Vocabulary Check:**

Draw a line from the word to its meaning.

| treat | | a furry brown and black animal |
|---|---|---|
| raccoon | | a small river |
| stream | | food; a snack |
| snatch | | feels for |
| paws | | take quickly |

**HOT Questions:**

1. Why do you think the raccoon climbed onto the rock? _____

2. Why do you think he dipped his paws in the stream? _____

3. Do you think he knows what he is looking for? Why or why not? _____

4. Why do you think he uses his paws and not his tail? _____

# 6 Jane Goodall

Jane Goodall studied chimpanzees in the jungle. At first, when the chimps saw the thin blonde woman, they ran away. In time, they let her get close to watch them eat and play. She even saw chimps make and use tools, like people do.

Sentence by Sentence
Date: _____

**Vocabulary to Visualize:**

**study:** look at and think about carefully
**chimpanzee:** an ape that has long brown hair covering most of its body
**blonde:** fair or light-colored hair
**tool:** a thing used to help when working

## A  Picture This: Jane Goodall studied chimpanzees in the jungle.

*Which best matches your picture?*  ○   ○

**Underline the answer that best matches your own picture.**

| | | | |
|---|---|---|---|
| 1. What did you picture for Jane? | a woman | a man | a child |
| 2. How did you see her studying the chimpanzees? | watching closely | reading a book | |
| 3. How did you picture the chimpanzees? | child-sized with arms and legs | bug-sized with tails | |
| 4. Where did you picture Jane and the chimpanzees? | in a jungle | in a city | in the snow |

**Did you picture all of the structure words?  Check each one you saw in your image.**
☐ What  ☐ Size  ☐ Color  ☐ Number  ☐ Shape  ☐ Where
☐ Movement  ☐ Mood  ☐ Background  ☐ Perspective  ☐ When  ☐ Sound

**Picture This:** At first, when the chimps saw the thin blonde woman, they ran away.

1. What did those words make you picture?   Jane chasing chimps   chimps running from Jane
2. What did you see for the chimps' mood?   happy   scared   angry
3. What color did you picture for Jane's hair? _____
4. How did you see the chimps running?   on two legs like a person   on four legs like a dog
5. Where did you see the chimps run to?   into the jungle   up Jane's leg   to the beach
6. Where did you see Jane when the chimps ran away?   standing with chimps   standing alone

**Picture This:** In time, they let her get close to watch them eat and play.

1. What did those words make you picture?   chimps hiding   Jane near chimps   Jane hiding
2. How did you see Jane get close?   walking slow   running fast   sitting down
3. How did you see the chimps eating?   with knives and forks   with their hands   with straws
4. How did you see them play?   they rolled around   they hit a ball   they dressed dolls
5. How did you see her watch the chimps?   looking at them   running from them

**Picture This:** She even saw chimps make and use tools, like people do.

*Which best matches your picture?*

Underline the answer that best matches your own picture.

1. What did you picture for the chimps' tools?   bulldozers   sticks
2. How did you see the chimps get the tools?   picked up off the ground   bought at the store
3. How did you see the chimps using the tools?   digging   throwing   scratching
4. Where did you see Jane?   watching from nearby   sleeping   helping the chimps

**Picture Summary:**
Number your images in order.

☐ The chimps ran away from the thin woman with blonde hair when she came to study them.

☐ Jane saw the chimps using their own tools, like people do.

☐ Jane Goodall went to watch chimps in the jungle and study them.

☐ The chimps let Jane near as they ate, and played after she had been there awhile.

**Word Summary:**
Fill in the blanks using the words listed below.

Jane Goodall _____ chimpanzees in the jungle. At first, the chimps _____ away from the blonde woman. In time, they let her watch them play and _____. She saw them make and use _____ just like humans do.

**ran      eat      studied      tools**

**Main Idea:**

Connect these with a line.

| | |
|---|---|
| Jane Goodall did not like to study chimps. | a detail |
| The chimps made and used tools. | main idea |
| Jane Goodall studied chimps in the jungle. | wrong |

**Vocabulary Check:**

Draw a line from the word to its meaning.

| | |
|---|---|
| study | ape that has hair over most of its body |
| blonde | a thing used to help when working |
| chimpanzee | to look at and think about carefully |
| jungle | a hot place with lots of plants and trees |
| tool | fair or light-colored hair |

**HOT Questions:**

1. Why do you think Jane wanted to study chimpanzees? _____

_____

2. Why do you think the chimps ran away when they first saw her? _____

_____

3. Why do you think it took time before the chimps let her get close to them? _____

_____

4. How do you think Jane felt when she saw the chimps use tools? _____

_____

# 7 Venus Flytrap

The Venus Flytrap is a swamp plant that eats bugs! Flies smell the sweet leaves and buzz in. When a fly lands on the open pair of leaves, they slam shut to trap the bug. Over the next few days, a juice from the leaves breaks down all but the fly's wings and legs.

**Sentence by Sentence**
Date: _____

**Vocabulary to Visualize:**

**Venus Flytrap:** a plant that has jaw-like leaves that can lose on a bug
**swamp:** an area of land with lots of water and plants in it
**pair:** two things that match
**trap:** catch

## A  Picture This: The Venus Flytrap is a swamp plant that eats bugs!

*Which best matches your picture?*   ○   ○

**Underline or write in the answer that best matches your own picture.**

| | | | |
|---|---|---|---|
| 1. How big was the flytrap you saw? | big as a tree | big as a flower | big as a person |
| 2. What color did you picture the plant? | _____ | | |
| 3. What did you see for the swamp? | soggy ground | dry ground | |
| 4. What did you see for bugs? | lions | people | flies |

**Did you picture all of the structure words? Check each one you saw in your image.**
☐ What  ☐ Size  ☐ Color  ☐ Number  ☐ Shape  ☐ Where
☐ Movement  ☐ Mood  ☐ Background  ☐ Perspective  ☐ When  ☐ Sound

**B** **Picture This:** Flies smell the sweet leaves and buzz in.

| | | | |
|---|---|---|---|
| 1. What did those words make you picture? | bugs flying to the plant | bugs flying away from the plant | |
| 2. How did you picture the flies? | crawling beetles | small bugs with wings | worms |
| 3. What color did you picture the flies? | _____ | | |
| 4. How big did you picture the plant leaves? | big as a fingertip | big as pancake | |
| 5. What shape did you picture the plant leaves? | square | round | rectangle |
| 6. How did you see the flies buzzing in? | flying slowly | flying quickly | |

**C** **Picture This:** When a fly lands on the open pair of leaves, they slam shut to trap the bug.

| | | | |
|---|---|---|---|
| 1. What did those words make you picture? | bug near plant | bug caught in plant | bug eating plant |
| 2. What did you see the leaves do? | fall | shake | close together |
| 3. What color did you picture the leaves? | _____ | | |
| 4. How did you see the fly land? | with its feet on a leaf | with its feet on the stem | |
| 5. How did you see that the fly was trapped? | stuck in the leaves | flying away from the leaves | |
| 6. How did you see the leaves close? | fast | slow | |

**Picture This:** Over the next few days, a juice from the leaves breaks down all but the fly's wings and legs.

*Which best matches your picture?*

○  ○

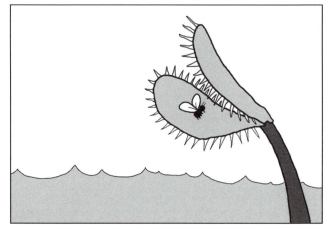

**Underline the answer that best matches your own picture.**

| | | | |
|---|---|---|---|
| **1.** What did you see happen to the fly? | juice melted the fly | | juice cleaned the fly |
| **2.** What did you see for the juice? | sticky slime | running water | dirty mud |
| **3.** Where did you see the juice come from? | inside the leaves | a bottle | a fruit |
| **4.** What parts of the fly did you see left in the flytrap? | wings and legs | | eyes and ears |

## Picture Summary:
Number your images in order.

☐ The Venus Flytrap was living in a swamp, eating bugs.

☐ Flies buzz toward the plant, getting close to it.

☐ A fly lands on a leaf and gets trapped when the leaves slam shut.

☐ The fly is melted by the plant's juice until only legs and wings are left.

## Word Summary:
Fill in the blanks using the words listed below.

The Venus Flytrap is a plant that eats _____.

In the swamp, flies _____ to the plant.

When a fly lands on the leaves, they close up and _____ it. A juice breaks down all but the _____ and legs over a few days.

**trap    buzz    wings    bugs**

**Main Idea:**

Connect these with a line.

| Venus Flytrap plants eat bugs. | a detail |
| The leaves have a sweet smell. | main idea |
| Venus Flytrap plants eat plants. | wrong |

**Vocabulary Check:**

Draw a line from the word to its meaning.

| swamp | a low humming sound |
| trap | to catch |
| fly | a plant that has leaves that can close on a bug |
| buzz | a small flying insect |
| Venus Flytrap | an area of land with lots of water and plants in it |

**HOT Questions:**

1. How do you think the leaves know when a fly has landed on it? _____

2. Why do you think the wings and legs are left over? _____

3. Why do you think this plant is called the flytrap? _____

4. Why do you think the flies go to the plant? _____

# 8 The Gecko

Sentence by Sentence
Date: _____

The gecko is a small bumpy-skinned lizard with big toes and eyes. Her toes have short, stiff hairs that help her cling to trees as she climbs. Her bulging eyes can see in the dark. She hunts at night, zipping up a tree to catch a bug.

**Vocabulary to Visualize:**

**gecko:** a small lizard with clingy toes and big eyes
**cling:** hold tightly
**bulging:** curved or sticking out
**zip:** move very fast

## A Picture This: The gecko is a small bumpy-skinned lizard with big toes and eyes.

*Which best matches your picture?*  ○  ○

**Underline or write in the answer that best matches your own picture.**

| | | | |
|---|---|---|---|
| **1.** What color did you picture for the gecko? | | | |
| **2.** How did you picture her skin? | hairy | rough | smooth |
| **3.** How big did you picture the gecko? | | big as a cat | big as a mouse |
| **4.** How big did you picture the bumps on her skin? | | big as hills | big as bug bites |

**Did you picture all of the structure words? Check each one you saw in your image.**
☐ What  ☐ Size  ☐ Color  ☐ Number  ☐ Shape  ☐ Where
☐ Movement  ☐ Mood  ☐ Background  ☐ Perspective  ☐ When  ☐ Sound

**B** **Picture This:** Her toes have short, stiff hairs that help her cling to trees as she climbs.

1. What did those words make you picture?   gecko toes with hairs   gecko ears with hairs
2. How did you picture the hairs?   thin and soft   short and hard
3. How many hairs did you see?   lots   a few   none
4. Where did you see the gecko?   on the ground   in a tree   in a car
5. How did you see her climb?   on her back legs only   on all four legs   on her front legs only

**C** **Picture This:** Her bulging eyes can see in the dark.

1. What did those words make you picture?   gecko at night   gecko during the day
2. What shape did you see for her eyes?   round   square   pointy
3. How did you see that her eyes were bulging?   they stuck out   they were flat
4. How did you see that it was dark?   no light   lots of sun   sun and clouds
5. What did you picture her seeing in the dark?   plants and bugs   movies
6. What did you picture her doing?   crawling on the ground   bumping into trees   climbing trees

**Picture This:** She hunts at night, zipping up a tree to catch a bug.

*Which best matches your picture?*   ◯   ◯

**Underline the answer that best matches your own picture.**

1. How did you picture the gecko hunting?     being fed     searching for food
2. What did you see her hunting?     a cat     a leaf     a bug
3. How did you see her "zipping?"     crawling fast     creeping
4. Where did you see the bug?     above her     below her     behind her

**Picture Summary:**
Number your images in order.

☐ The gecko ran up a tree to catch and eat a bug.

☐ The gecko lizard has bumpy skin, big eyes, and big toes.

☐ The gecko has toes with short hairs to help her cling to trees.

☐ The gecko has bulging eyes that can see in the dark, so she hunts at night.

**Word Summary:**
Fill in the blanks using the words listed below.

The gecko is a lizard with bumpy _____.

She has big toes and eyes. Her _____ have short _____ to help her cling to trees. Her big eyes _____ in the dark. She hunts at night, zipping after bugs.

**toes     skin     hairs     see**

**Main Idea:**

Connect these with a line.

| | |
|---|---|
| Geckos have eyes and toes that help them hunt. | a detail |
| Geckos have ears and hands that help them hunt. | main idea |
| Geckos zip up a tree. | wrong |

**Vocabulary Check:**

Draw a line from the word to its meaning.

| | |
|---|---|
| zip | a four-legged reptile |
| lizard | curved or sticking out |
| cling | a small lizard with clingy toes and big eyes |
| gecko | move very fast |
| bulging | hold tightly |

**HOT Questions:**

1. What part of her toes do you think the short stiff hairs are on? _____

2. What do you think would happen if her toes were hairless? _____

3. What do you think might happen if she had small, flat eyes? _____

4. Why do you think it's important that she can climb the tree quickly? _____

# 9 Prickly Pear Snack

The fruit of a prickly pear cactus is spiked with thin needles. When a hiker finds the cactus, he plucks the red fruit off with two sharp sticks. He peels off its skin with a knife. Then he pops the sweet fruit into his mouth for a snack.

Sentence by Sentence
Date: _____

**Vocabulary to Visualize:**

**prickly pear:** a cactus with flat stems and round fruit
**needle:** a thin, sharp spike that grows from a plant, like a thorn
**pluck:** grab quickly
**peel:** cut away the skin of a fruit or vegetable

## A. Picture This: The fruit of a prickly pear cactus is spiked with thin needles.

*Which best matches your picture?*  ◯   ◯

**Underline or write in the answer that best matches your own picture.**

| | | | |
|---|---|---|---|
| **1.** What color did you picture the cactus? | | | |
| **2.** Where did you see the fruit on the cactus? | on the sides | on the top | on the bottom |
| **3.** What did you see for the needles on the fruit? | thin spikes | flat leaves | thick twigs |
| **4.** Where did you see the needles? | on top of the fruit | all over the fruit | |

**Did you picture all of the structure words? Check each one you saw in your image.**
☐ What  ☐ Size  ☐ Color  ☐ Number  ☐ Shape  ☐ Where
☐ Movement  ☐ Mood  ☐ Background  ☐ Perspective  ☐ When  ☐ Sound

**B** **Picture This:** When a hiker finds the cactus, he plucks the red fruit off with two sharp sticks.

| | | | |
|---|---|---|---|
| 1. | What did those words make you picture? | hiker picking fruit | hiker crushing fruit |
| 2. | How did you picture him finding the cactus? | seeing it | not seeing it |
| 3. | How did you see him picking the fruit? | with thin twigs | with two baseball bats |
| 4. | What color did you picture the fruit? | _____ | |
| 5. | What did you see him do with the sticks? | knock the fruit off | pinch the fruit off |
| 6. | How did you see that the sticks were sharp? | rounded ends | pointy ends |

**C** **Picture This:** He peels off its skin with a knife.

| | | | | |
|---|---|---|---|---|
| 1. | What did those words make you picture? | hiker throwing fruit | hiker peeling off skin of fruit | |
| 2. | How did you see him holding the knife? | with his hand | with his foot | with his arms |
| 3. | Where did you see him get the knife from? | the ground | a tree | his pack |
| 4. | How did you see the skin before he peeled it? | thick and bumpy | thin and prickly | |
| 5. | How did you see him peel the fruit? | cut with knife | rip with hands | carve with fingernails |
| 6. | What did you see for the peeled fruit? | rough and hard | prickly | smooth |

**D** **Picture This:** Then he pops the sweet fruit into his mouth for a snack.

*Which best matches your picture?*

Underline or write in the answer that best matches your own picture.

1. How did you see the hiker putting the fruit in his mouth?   quickly   slowly
2. How did you picture his mouth when he put the fruit in?   open   closed   frowning
3. How did you see him eating the fruit?   little bites   all at once
4. What shape did you picture the fruit? _____

**Picture Summary:**
Number your images in order.

- The hiker ate the sweet fruit now that the skin was off.
- A hiker used two sticks to pick the prickly fruit off the cactus.
- The hiker peeled off the skin from the fruit with his knife.
- A prickly pear cactus has round fruit with sharp needles.

**Word Summary:**
Fill in the blanks using the words listed below.

The prickly pear cactus has fruit with _____ all over it. When a hiker finds the cactus, he picks a piece of _____ with two sticks. Then he takes out his knife and _____ off the spiky skin before popping the fruit into his _____.

**peels**   **needles**   **mouth**   **fruit**

38

**Main Idea:**

Connect these with a line.

| | |
|---|---|
| The fruit of the prickly pear can be eaten without its needles. | a detail |
| The prickly pear's fruit is red. | main idea |
| The fruit of the prickly pear can be eaten with its needles. | wrong |

**Vocabulary Check:**

Draw a line from the word to its meaning.

| | |
|---|---|
| prickly pear | a plant with no leaves, only stems and branches |
| peel | grab quickly |
| pluck | cut away the skin of a fruit or vegetable |
| cactus | a sharp, thin spike |
| needle | a cactus with flat stems and round fruit |

**HOT Questions:**

1. Why do you think the hiker plucks the fruit with sticks? Why not use his fingers? _____

2. Why do you think the hiker peels off the fruit's skin? _____

3. Why would a hiker want to eat the fruit of this cactus? _____

4. Why do you think it is called the prickly pear cactus? _____

# 10 King Tut

Long ago, King Tut ruled Egypt. When he died at a young age, he was put in an underground tomb with many rooms. Each room was lit with lamps and filled with Tut's treasures. The rooms were crammed with gold, jewels, food, and games.

**Sentence by Sentence**
Date: _____

**Vocabulary to Visualize:**

**rule:** lead; control
**Egypt:** an ancient country in Africa known for its great stone pyramids and temples
**tomb:** a place to bury the dead; a grave
**treasure:** things of great wealth or importance
**cram:** fill too tightly; over full

## A  Picture This: Long ago, King Tut ruled Egypt.

*Which best matches your picture?*  ○  ○

**Underline the answer that best matches your own picture.**

| | | | |
|---|---|---|---|
| 1. How did you see Tut ruling? | giving orders | taking orders | getting yelled at |
| 2. When did you see him ruling? | before there were cars | after there were cars | |
| 3. What did you see for Egypt? | a big kingdom | a small town | a school |
| 4. Where did you picture Egypt? | in the warm desert | in the cold snow | in the wet jungle |

**Did you picture all of the structure words? Check each one you saw in your image.**
☐ What  ☐ Size  ☐ Color  ☐ Number  ☐ Shape  ☐ Where
☐ Movement  ☐ Mood  ☐ Background  ☐ Perspective  ☐ When  ☐ Sound

**B** **Picture This:** When he died at a young age, he was put in an underground tomb with many rooms.

| | | | |
|---|---|---|---|
| 1. What did those words make you picture? | Tut on a throne | Tut in a grave | Tut at a party |
| 2. How old did you picture him? | _____ years old | | |
| 3. How did you see him as dead? | still and eyes closed | laughing | breathing and eyes closed |
| 4. What did you picture for his tomb? | muddy hole | rooms with stone walls | |
| 5. Where did you see his tomb? | below the ground | on top of a mountain | |
| 6. How did you see him being put in the tomb? | walking | crawling | being carried |

**C** **Picture This:** Each room was lit with lamps and filled with Tut's treasures.

| | | | |
|---|---|---|---|
| 1. What did those words make you picture? | rooms with riches | empty rooms | |
| 2. How did you see the rooms? | dark | lit by sun | lit by lamps |
| 3. What did you see for the lamps? | small lights | headlights | light bulbs |
| 4. What color did you picture the lamp light? | yellow | black | blue |
| 5. How did you picture the treasures? | coins and jewels | old boots | |
| 6. Where did you see Tut's treasures? | on the walls | on the floor | on the ceiling |

**D** **Picture This:** The rooms were crammed with gold, jewels, food, and games.

*Which best matches your picture?*  ○   ○

**Underline the answer that best matches your own picture.**

1. Where did you see Tut?     in the room with treasures     outside the room with treasures
2. How did you see that the rooms were crammed with treasures?   treasure everywhere   treasure in a pile
3. What did you see for gold?     rocks     fish     necklaces and rings
4. What did you see for jewels?     shiny stones     rough paper

**Picture Summary:**
Number your images in order.

- King Tut ruled Egypt before he died at a young age.
- King Tut's tomb had lots of games, food, gold, and jewels.
- King Tut was buried in an underground tomb with many rooms.
- King Tut's tomb was lit with many lamps.

**Word Summary:**
Fill in the blanks using the words listed below.

King Tut _____ at a young age. He was put into an underground _____ with many rooms. The rooms were filled with treasure, _____, games, and more. They also had _____, which were lit, and food.

**gold     tomb     lamps     died**

**Main Idea:**
Connect these with a line.

| | |
|---|---|
| King Tut was buried in a tomb with many rooms filled with his stuff. | a detail |
| King Tut was buried in a tomb with one empty room. | main idea |
| King Tut had treasures like gold and jewels. | wrong |

**Vocabulary Check:**
Draw a line from the word to its meaning.

| | |
|---|---|
| tomb | ancient country in Africa known for pyramids |
| cram | things of great value or importance |
| Egypt | lead; control |
| rule | fill too tightly; overfull |
| treasure | a place to bury the dead; a grave |

**HOT Questions:**

1. Why do you think King Tut was buried with his treasures? _____

2. Why do you think he was buried with games? _____

3. Why do you think he died when he was still young? _____

4. Why do you think the rooms were lit with lamps? Why would it be important for the rooms to have light? _____

# 11 The Jump

Multiple Sentence
Date: _____

The girl rode her horse to the field. She looked at a stone fence and wondered if they could jump over it. The horse ran straight toward the fence. When they got close, he leaped, and they sailed over the rails.

**Vocabulary to Visualize:**

**stone fence:** two brick towers with wooden rails between them
**wonder:** think about
**leap:** jump
**sail:** fly or glide through the air
**rail:** wooden beam or log

**A  Picture This:** The girl rode her horse to the field. She looked at a stone fence and wondered if they could jump over it.

Underline or write in the answer that best matches your own picture.

| | | | | |
|---|---|---|---|---|
| 1. | What did those words make you picture? | a girl on a horse | a girl on a dog | |
| 2. | What did you see the girl doing? | thinking about a jump | thinking about lunch | |
| 3. | Where did you see the girl and the horse? | in the park | in the mall | in the field |
| 4. | What did you see the girl wearing? | a swimsuit | a crown | pants and a shirt |
| 5. | What color did you picture the horse? _____ | | | |
| 6. | How did you see her looking at the fence? | she faced the fence | she closed her eyes | she covered her face |
| 7. | How did you picture the fence? | tall as a book | tall as a table | tall as a skyscraper |
| 8. | What did you picture for the fence? | rocks stacked up | hay tied together | |

**B** **Picture This:** The horse ran straight toward the fence. When they got close, he leaped, and they sailed over the rails.

Underline the answer that best matches your own picture.

1. What did those words make you picture?   girl and horse going over a fence   girl feeding a horse
2. How did you see the horse get to the fence?   it ran fast   it walked slowly   it reared up
3. How did you see that the horse went toward the fence?   ran closer to the fence   ran away from the fence
4. How did you see the horse leaping?   jumped high off the ground   dug into the ground
5. How quickly did you see the horse leap?   in seconds   in hours   in years
6. What did you see the girl do when the horse leaped?   put her hands in air   leaned down and held on tight
7. Where did you see the fence when they sailed over it?   under them   away from them   over them

**Picture Summary:**

Number these pictures in order:

**Word Summary:**
Fill in the blanks using the words listed below.

The girl _____ her horse to the field where she sat and looked at the stone fence. She wondered if they could _____ over it. Then the horse _____ , heading for the fence. When they were close, the horse leaped, and they sailed over the _____ .

**rails**  **rode**  **jump**  **ran**

**Main Idea:**
Connect these with a line.

| The horse ran toward the fence. | a detail |
| The girl and the horse jumped under the fence. | main idea |
| The girl and the horse jumped over the fence. | wrong |

**Spelling Practice:**
Trace then cover the word.   Air-write then pencil write the word.

wonder

horse

**Vocabulary Check:**
Draw a line from the word to its meaning.

| rail | think about |
| wonder | wooden beam or log |
| leap | two towers with rails between them |
| stone fence | fly or glide through the air |
| sail | jump |

**HOT Questions:**

**1.** Do you think the girl wanted her horse to run at the wall?  Why or why not? _____

_____

**2.** What might happen if the horse leaped at the wrong time? _____

_____

**3.** How do you think the girl felt when her horse started to run? _____

_____

**4.** Why do you think the girl was not sure if they could jump over the stone fence? _____

_____

**Vocabulary Fun:**

Color the picture that best matches the word.

# 12  Koala

Multiple Sentence
Date: _____

The soft gray koala climbs through the trees at night.  Her strong grip and sharp claws hold her tight to the high branches.  She chews off the long, green water-filled leaves.  When the sun comes up, she hides in the shade and sleeps.

**Vocabulary to Visualize:**
**koala:** gray, furry, bear-like animal that lives in Australia
**claw:** a sharp curved thing on an animal's toe
**grip:** a strong hold
**shade:** a dark place out of or blocked from sunlight

## A  Picture This: The soft gray koala climbs through the trees at night.  Her strong grip and sharp claws hold her tight to the high branches.

Underline or write in the answer that best matches your own picture.

| | | | |
|---|---|---|---|
| 1. | What did those words make you picture? | koala high in trees | koala crawling on ground |
| 2. | Where did you see the koala? | on the tree branches | stuck to the tree trunk |
| 3. | How did you see that she climbs through the trees? | moves from branch to branch | slides down the trunk |
| 4. | How did you see that it was night? | sun in the sky | no sun in the sky |
| 5. | What shape did you picture the koala? | skinny | round and plump |
| 6. | What color did you picture the koala? _____ | | |
| 7. | How did you see that she had a strong grip on the branch? | she held on tight | she fell out of the tree |
| 8. | How did you see her sharp claws on the branch? | they slip off the branch | they cut into the branch |

**B** **Picture This:** She chews off the long, green water-filled leaves. When the sun comes up, she hides in the shade and sleeps.

Underline or write in the answer that best matches your own picture.

| | | | |
|---|---|---|---|
| 1. | What did those words make you picture? | koala eating and sleeping | koala living in the ocean |
| 2. | How did you see the koala eating? | munching on leaves | licking the bark |
| 3. | Where did you picture the leaves? | on the ground | on the branches |
| 4. | What color did you picture the leaves? | | |
| 5. | How did you see that the sun came up? | dark sky became light | light sky became dark |
| 6. | How did you see the koala hide? | she went under some leaves | she went above the leaves |
| 7. | How did you picture the koala sleeping? | eyes closed, breathing softly | eyes open, and singing loudly |

**Picture Summary:**

Number these pictures in order:

**Word Summary:**
Fill in the blanks using the words listed below.

The gray koala climbed through the _____

at night. Her strong _____ and sharp claws

held her tight to the high branches. She chewed long,

green water-filled _____ . When the sun

came up, she hid in the shade to _____ .

**grip**  **sleep**  **trees**  **leaves**

**Main Idea:**
Connect these with a line.

| Koalas live, eat, and sleep high in trees. | a detail |
| Koalas have sharp claws. | main idea |
| Koalas live, eat, and sleep in caves. | wrong |

**Spelling Practice:**
Trace then cover the word.    Air-write then pencil write the word.

climb

through

**Vocabulary Check:**
Draw a line from the word to its meaning.

| shade | a sharp curved thing on an animal's toe |
| koala | a strong hold |
| grip | move out of sight |
| hide | gray, furry, bear-like animal |
| claw | a dark place out of sunlight |

**HOT Questions:**

1. How do you think her sharp claws help her hold tight to the branches? _____
_____

2. What might happen if the koala didn't hold tight to the branches? _____
_____

3. Do you think the koala has to leave the trees to find water? Explain. _____
_____

4. Do you think the koala likes the day or night better? Why? _____
_____

**Vocabulary Fun:**

Color the picture that best matches the word.

| koala | claw | leaves |

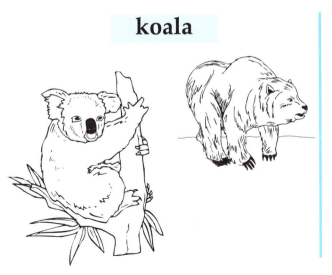
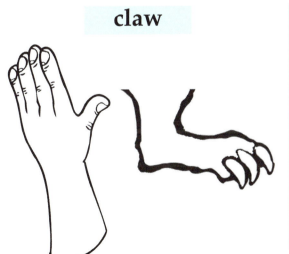
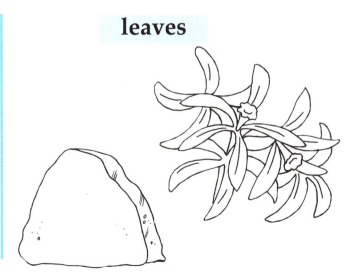

# 13 Target Practice

Multiple Sentence
Date: _____

The young girl grabbed her bow and arrow. She faced the round paper target on the bale of hay. She aimed for the center of the target and shot. The arrow flew and hit the bull's eye.

**Vocabulary to Visualize:**

**bow:** a curved piece of wood and a string used to shoot arrows
**arrow:** a long stick with a point on one end and feathers on the other
**target:** an object or point to aim at
**bale of hay:** a bunch of dried grass shaped and tied into a rectangle
**bull's eye:** the center of a target

## A  Picture This: The young girl grabbed her bow and arrow. She faced the round paper target on the bale of hay.

Underline or write in the answer that best matches your own picture.

1. What did those words make you picture?   a girl getting ready to shoot   a girl getting ready for a party
2. How did you see that she grabbed her bow and arrow?   picked them up with hands   kicked with feet
3. What did you see for the bow?   long curved piece of wood with a cord   round metal ball
4. What color did you picture the bow? _____
5. Where on the bow did you see the string?   from one end to the other   tangled around it
6. What shape did you see for the tip of the arrow?   round   square   pointed
7. How did you see that she faced the paper target?   looking at bale of hay   looking away from bale of hay
8. What did you see on the paper target?   painted-on circles   painted-on squares

**Picture This:** She aimed for the center of the target and shot. The arrow flew and hit the bull's eye.

Underline or write in the answer that best matches your own picture.

1. What did those words make you picture?    girl shooting at target    girl shooting at a can
2. How did you see her aiming?    she pointed the arrow at the target    she pointed the arrow at the sky
3. How did you see that the arrow flew?    went through air    slid on the ground
4. Where did you see the center of the target?    inside the other circles    in the corner of the paper
5. What color did you picture for the center of the target? _____
6. What size did you picture the center    small as a dime    big as a tire
7. How did you see that the arrow hit the target?    stuck in the middle    bounced off the edge

## Picture Summary:

Number these pictures in order:

**Word Summary:**
Fill in the blanks using the words listed below.

The young girl grabbed her _____ and arrow. She stood facing the round paper target on the _____ of hay. She aimed carefully for the center of the target and _____ . The arrow sailed through the air and landed right in the bull's _____ .

**shot        bale        eye        bow**

**Main Idea:**
Connect these with a line.

| A girl shot an arrow at the target and missed the center. | a detail |
| A girl shot an arrow at the target and hit the center. | main idea |
| A girl grabbed her bow and arrow. | wrong |

**Spelling Practice:**
Trace then cover the word.     Air-write then pencil write the word.

paper

center

**Vocabulary Check:**
Draw a line from the word to its meaning.

| bale of hay | dried grass tied into a rectangle shape |
| arrow | an object or point to aim at |
| bull's eye | a long stick with a point and feathers |
| target | the center of a target |
| bow | a curved piece of wood and a string |

**HOT Questions:**

1. Why do you think she aimed for the center of the target? _____

2. How do you think the girl felt when she hit the center of the target? _____

3. Why do you think targets are placed on bales of hay? _____

4. What do you think the center of the target is called? _____

**Vocabulary Fun:**

Color the picture that best matches the word.

| bow and arrow | target | bales of hay |

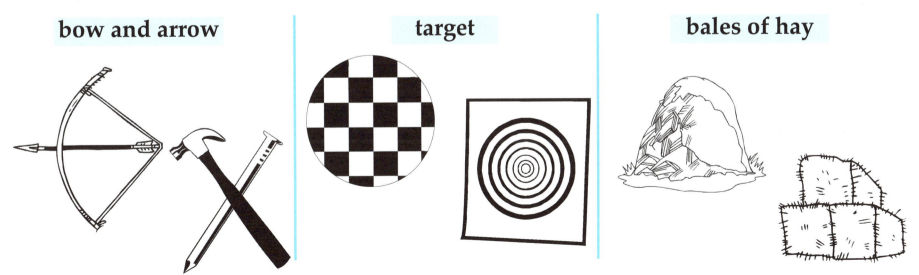

# 14 The Sheep Herder

**Multiple Sentence**
Date: _____

The brown and white collie ran to the sheep in the field. She barked at the sheep and nipped at their fur. She forced them to huddle close. She kept the scared sheep in a tight bunch until her master arrived.

**Vocabulary to Visualize:**

**collie:** a smart dog used for herding
**nip:** bite suddenly and lightly
**huddle:** to crowd close together
**bunch:** a group of things
**master:** boss; owner

## A

**Picture This:** The brown and white collie ran to the sheep in the field. She barked at the sheep and nipped at their fur.

Underline or write in the answer that best matches your own picture.

1. What did those words make you picture?     a dog herding sheep    a dog herding cows
2. How did you picture the collie's fur?    long and straight    short and curly    short and straight
3. What color did you picture the collie's fur? _____
4. How did you picture the collie running?    slow    fast
5. How did you see her barking?    mouth open    mouth closed
6. How did you picture that she nipped at the sheep?    little bites that scared them    sharp bites that hurt them
7. What color did you picture the sheep? _____
8. How many sheep did you picture?    one    two    twenty

**B** **Picture This:** She forced them to huddle close. She kept the scared sheep in a tight bunch until her master arrived.

Underline the answer that best matches your own picture.

| | | | |
|---|---|---|---|
| 1. | What did those words make you picture? | a dog attacking sheep | a dog running around sheep |
| 2. | How did you see her making the sheep stay close? | forcing them together | pushing them apart |
| 3. | How did you picture the sheep huddling? | close to each other | on different hills |
| 4. | How did you see that the sheep were scared? | laughing | crying |
| 5. | How did you picture the tight bunch? | space between each sheep | sheep standing close together |
| 6. | What did you picture for the master? | an adult | a child |
| 7. | How did you see the master arriving? | drove up in a car | walked up | fell from the sky |

**Picture Summary:**

Number these pictures in order:

## Word Summary:
Fill in the blanks using the words listed below.

The brown and white collie _____ to the sheep in the field. She barked at the _____ and nipped at their _____. She forced them to huddle close. She kept the scared sheep in a tight _____ until her master arrived.

**ran    fur    sheep    bunch**

## Main Idea:
Connect these with a line.

| The collie nipped at the sheep's fur. | a detail |
| The collie scared the sheep away. | main idea |
| The collie herded the sheep into a bunch. | wrong |

## Spelling Practice:
Trace then cover the word.    Air-write then pencil write the word.

barked

forced

## Vocabulary Check:
Draw a line from the word to its meaning.

| bunch | a smart dog used for herding |
| collie | a group of things |
| sheep | bite suddenly and lightly |
| master | four-legged animals with thick fluffy fur |
| nip | boss; owner |

**HOT Questions:**

1. How do you think the collie forced the sheep into a huddle? _____

2. Why do you think the sheep were scared? _____

3. What do you think will happen next? _____

4. Why do you think the master uses the dog to herd sheep? _____

**Vocabulary Fun:**

Color the picture that best matches the word.

| collie | bunch | sheep |

# 15 Tornado

The dark funnel cloud dropped from the sky and touched down near a small house. The wind in the funnel roared as it spun in circles. The house shook as the twister got close. The twister smashed into the house, flinging wood and bricks.

**Multiple Sentence**
Date: _____

**Vocabulary to Visualize:**
**tornado:** a spinning, cone-shaped storm of wind and debris
**funnel:** a cone with a wide opening leading to a narrow tip
**roar:** make a loud, deep sound
**spun:** went around in a circle over and over very fast
**fling:** throw wildly

## A

**Picture This:** The dark funnel cloud dropped from the sky and touched down near a small house. The wind in the funnel roared as it spun in circles.

Underline or write in the answer that best matches your own picture.

1. What did those words make you picture?    tornado near a house    tornado near a boat
2. How did you picture the tornado?    a cloud of spinning wind    a flash of lightning    earth splitting open
3. What shape did you picture the tornado?    square    cone
4. What color did you picture the tornado? _____
5. How did you see that the tornado was near the house?    cloud far away from house    cloud close to house
6. What color did you picture the house? _____
7. How did you picture that the house was small?    lots of windows and doors    just a few windows and doors
8. How did you hear the wind roaring?    loud and low    soft and high
9. How did you see that the wind spun in circles?    it went round and round    it went up and down

**Picture This:** The house shook as the twister got close. The twister smashed into the house, flinging wood and bricks.

Underline the answer that best matches your own picture.

1. What did those words make you picture?   tornado destroying house   tornado building house
2. How did you see the house shaking before the tornado hit it?   walls rattled   walls stayed still
3. How did you see the twister smashing into the house?   funnel cloud hit house   puffy cloud hit house
4. What part of the house did you see the twister hit first?   the front   the side   the back
5. How did you see that the house was smashed?   it broke into lots of pieces   it broke into two parts
6. How did you see the twister flinging wood and bricks?   they shot away   they stacked neatly
7. What did you see for the shape of the bricks?   rectangles   circles   triangles

## Picture Summary:
Number these pictures in order:

**Word Summary:**
Fill in the blanks using the words listed below.

The _____ , shaped like a funnel, dropped from the sky and touched down near a little house. The wind in the funnel roared as it _____ in circles. The house _____ as the twister got near. The twister smashed into the house, throwing bricks and _____ everywhere.

**spun**      **wood**      **cloud**      **shook**

**Main Idea:**
Connect these with a line.

| | |
|---|---|
| The tornado shook apart a house. | a detail |
| The tornado spun fast. | main idea |
| The tornado put together a house. | wrong |

**Spelling Practice:**
Trace then cover the word.      Air-write then pencil write the word.

touch

twister

**Vocabulary Check:**
Draw a line from the word to its meaning.

| | |
|---|---|
| tornado | cone shaped like an ice cream cone |
| spun | land on the ground |
| funnel | make a loud, deep sound |
| touch down | a spinning, cone-shaped storm |
| roar | went around in a circle very fast |

**HOT Questions:**

1. Do you think the wind in the funnel is blowing fast or slow? Why? _____
_____

2. Why do you think the house started to shake? _____
_____

3. What parts of the house do you think are left after the tornado passed? _____
_____

4. Where do you think the people of the house were? _____
_____

**Vocabulary Fun:**

Color the picture that best matches the word.

| tornado | funnel | bricks |
|---|---|---|
|  |  | 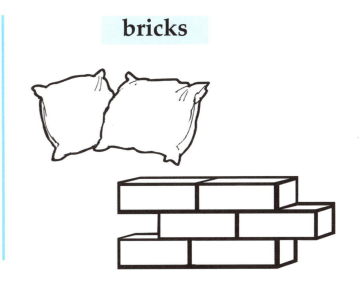 |

# 16  Kelp Forest

**Multiple Sentence**
Date: _____

Brown kelp forests live under the sea. The thick stalks grow air-filled bulbs that rise to the top of the water. The branches and leaves at the surface soak up the warm sunlight. This forest is a place where fish can live and hide.

**Vocabulary to Visualize:**
**kelp:** large plants that grow in the ocean
**stalk:** a plant stem
**bulb:** a round empty part of a plant
**surface:** the top of something
**soak:** take in

## A  Picture This:
Brown kelp forests live under the sea. The thick stalks grow air-filled bulbs that rise to the top of the water.

Underline or write in the answer that best matches your own picture.

1. What did those words make you picture?   seaweed in the ocean    seaweed in a fish tank
2. What did the kelp look like?    underwater trees    underwater flowers    underwater grass
3. How did you see that the kelp grew in a forest?    one kelp plant    lots of kelp plants close together
4. What color did you picture the kelp? _____
5. Where did you see the kelp plants grow from?    the top of the water    the ocean floor    top of a jelly fish
6. How thick did you picture the stalk?    thick as an arm    thick as an elephant    skinny as a pencil
7. How did you picture it growing?    to the top of the water    to the sandy bottom
8. What did you picture the air-filled bulbs doing?    pulling the plant up    sinking the plant

**B** **Picture This:** The branches and leaves at the surface soak up the warm sunlight. This forest is a place where fish can live and hide.

Underline the answer that best matches your own picture.

1. What did those words make you picture?                kelp with fish            kelp with divers
2. What did you see for the kelp's branches?            grew from the sand      grew from the stalk
3. What shape did you see for the kelp's leaves?        like fingers              like pancakes
4. What did the sunlight look like?                     rays shining down        rain falling
5. How did you see that some branches soak up sunlight?  grew toward floor      grew toward the ocean top
6. How many fish did you see?           lots        none        two
7. How did you see the fish hiding in the kelp?         under leaves            out in the open

**Picture Summary:**
Number these pictures in order:

**Word Summary:**
Fill in the blanks using the words listed below.

Brown _____ forests grow under the sea.

The thick stalks grow air-filled _____ that

rise to the top of the water. The branches and leaves

at the surface _____ up the warm sunlight.

This forest is a place where _____ can live

and hide.

**bulbs**      **kelp**      **fish**      **soak**

**Main Idea:**
Connect these with a line.

| | |
|---|---|
| Kelp forests grow air-filled bulbs that rise to the surface. | a detail |
| Kelp plants grow like forests in the sea. | main idea |
| Kelp plants grow like cacti in the desert. | wrong |

**Spelling Practice:**
Trace then cover the word.      Air-write then pencil write the word.

# forest

# branch

**Vocabulary Check:**
Draw a line from the word to its meaning.

| | |
|---|---|
| surface | a plant stem |
| kelp | a round empty part of a plant |
| soak | large plants that grow in the ocean |
| bulb | the top of something |
| stalk | take in |

**HOT Questions:**

1. Do you think the sea is shallow or deep where kelp grows?  Explain. _____
_____

2. Why do you think the kelp soaks up the sunlight? _____
_____

3. What do you think might happen to the stalks if they didn't have the air-filled bulbs? _____
_____

4. Why do you think fish live in the kelp forest? _____
_____

**Vocabulary Fun:**

Color the picture that best matches the word.

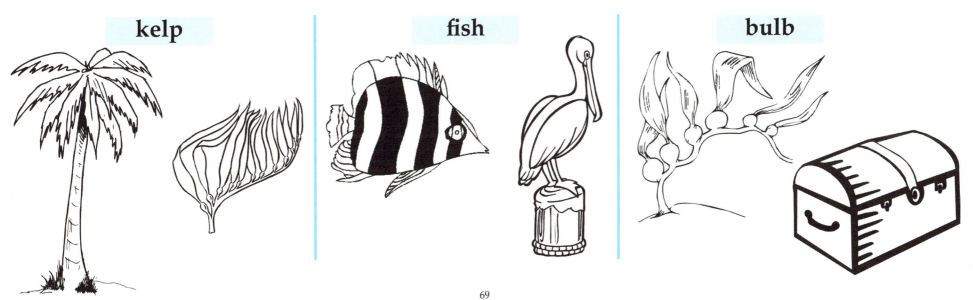

# 17 Snow Leopard

Multiple Sentence
Date: _____

The snow leopard crouches low to the ground with her gaze fixed on a mountain goat. Her light-colored fur with black spots blends in with the snow and rocks. In a flash, she leaps in the air and lands on the surprised goat. Then she eats her first meal in days.

**Vocabulary to Visualize:**
**leopard:** a large cat with spotted fur
**crouch:** bend low to the ground
**blend in:** to hide by looking like the things around it
**mountain goat:** a fluffy, four-legged animal with horns that lives on steep mountains

## A. Picture This:
The snow leopard crouches low to the ground with her gaze fixed on a mountain goat. Her light-colored fur with black spots blends in with the snow and rocks.

Underline or write in the answer that best matches your own picture.

1. What did those words make you picture?   leopard staring at a goat   leopard running away from a goat
2. How did you see that she was crouching?   her knees were bent   she stood tall on her back legs
3. How did you picture the leopard?   like a big cat   like a fluffy dog   like a little bird
4. What did you picture for the color of the leopard's fur?   white or tan with black spots   black with white spots
5. Where did you picture the leopard?   warm desert   mountain   forest
6. What did you see around the leopard?   cars and bikes   snow and rocks   flowers and bushes
7. What color did you picture the snow? _____
8. How did you see that she blends in?   hard to see her in snow   easy to see her in snow

**Picture This:** In a flash, she leaps in the air and lands on the surprised goat. Then she eats her first meal in days.

Underline the answer that best matches your own picture.

1. What did those words make you picture?   leopard killing goat   leopard running away from goat
2. How did you see the leopard attacking?   jumping on the goat   playing with the goat
3. Where did you see her jumping from?   behind the goat   in front of the goat
4. What part of the goat did you see her jumping on?   its back   its head
5. How many goats did you see?   one goat   many goats
6. What did you see happen to the goat?   it was eaten   it went swimming   it ate the leopard
7. How did the leopard feel after her meal?   hungry   full

**Picture Summary:**

Number these pictures in order:

**Word Summary:**
Fill in the blanks using the words listed below.

The snow leopard crouched _____ to the ground with her eyes fixed on a mountain goat. Her light-colored _____ with black spots blended in with white snow and rocks. Quickly, she _____ in the air and pounced on the goat. Then she _____ her first meal in days.

**fur          low          ate          jumped**

**Main Idea:**
Connect these with a line.

| The snow leopard caught a goat. | a detail |
| The snow leopard crouches low to the ground. | main idea |
| The snow leopard played with a goat. | wrong |

**Spelling Practice:**
Trace then cover the word.    Air-write then pencil write the word.

blends

first

**Vocabulary Check:**
Draw a line from the word to its meaning.

| leopard | a white layer of frozen flakes |
| crouch | a fluffy, four-legged animal with horns |
| goat | to look like the things around it |
| snow | bend low to the ground |
| blend in | a large cat with spotted fur |

**HOT Questions:**

1. Why do you think the leopard crouched low to the ground? _____

_____

2. How do you think the leopard felt, since she hadn't eaten in days? _____

_____

3. Why do you think the goat was surprised by the attack? _____

_____

4. Do you think the leopard would hunt this easily in a jungle? Explain. _____

_____

**Vocabulary Fun:**

Color the picture that best matches the word.

# 18 Locusts

A huge swarm of locusts flies over the cornfield. The hungry bugs land on, and crawl all over, the corn plants. They eat each green leaf, stalk, and ear of corn. Once they eat the plants to the ground, the bugs fly back up in the sky.

Multiple Sentence
Date: _____

**Vocabulary to Visualize:**

**swarm:** a large number of bugs or birds
**locust:** a type of grasshopper
**cornfield:** a place where corn is planted and grown
**stalk:** a plant's stem
**ear of corn:** the fruit of the corn plant that grows on a hard round cob

## A  Picture This: A huge swarm of locusts flies over the cornfield. The hungry bugs land on, and crawl all over, the corn plants.

Underline the answer that best matches your own picture.

1. What did those words make you picture?   locusts leaving a cornfield   locusts going into a cornfield
2. How did you see the locusts going into the cornfield?   running   flying   dancing
3. How did you see that the locusts fly in a swarm?   lots of bugs all together   a few bugs spread apart
4. What sound did you hear when you pictured the huge swarm flying?   loud bells   loud buzzing
5. How did you picture the cornfield?   rows of plants   just a few plants   no plants
6. Where did you see the locusts land?   on the corn plants   on the rocks   on the trees
7. What parts of the corn did you see them crawl over?   stalks, leaves, and corn   stalks only   corn only
8. How did you picture the corn when they were on it?   bugs moving all over it   one bug on each plant

**Picture This:** They eat each green leaf, stalk, and ear of corn. Once they eat the plants to the ground, the bugs fly back up in the sky.

Underline or write in the answer that best matches your own picture.

1. What did those words make you picture?    locusts destroy a field of corn    locusts plant a field of corn
2. How did you see the locusts eating the corn plants?    they ate all the plants    they ate the leaves only
3. What colors did you picture the corn plants? _____
4. What did you see on the ground when the bugs flew away?    lots of healthy plants    bits of plants
5. What did you see happen after they ate all the plants?    locusts danced    locusts flew
6. Where did you see the locusts fly?    away from the field    to the field    under the field
7. How many of them did you see flying away?    one of them    all of them    half of them

**Picture Summary:**

Number these pictures in order:

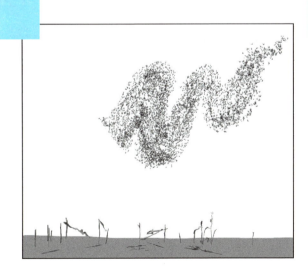
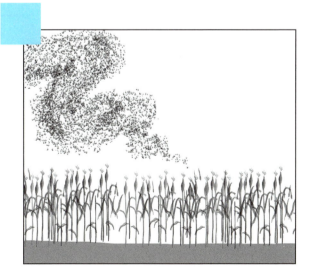

**Word Summary:**
Fill in the blanks using the words listed below.

A huge swarm of locusts flew over the cornfield. The hungry _____ landed and crawled on the corn plants. They _____ each green leaf, ear, and _____ of corn. When they flew off, the plants had been eaten to the _____ .

**ate**      **bugs**      **stalk**      **ground**

**Main Idea:**
Connect these with a line.

| The locusts flew in a swarm. | a detail |
| A swarm of locusts planted a cornfield in the ground. | main idea |
| A swarm of locusts ate a cornfield to the ground. | wrong |

**Spelling Practice:**
Trace then cover the word.     Air-write then pencil write the word.

plant

ground

**Vocabulary Check:**
Draw a line from the word to its meaning.

| stalk | a large number of bugs or birds |
| locust | a place where corn is grown |
| swarm | a type of grasshopper |
| huge | very big |
| cornfield | a plant's stem |

**HOT Questions:**

1. Why do you think the locusts chose that cornfield? _____
   _____

2. Do you think there were a lot of locusts? Why or why not? _____
   _____

3. Why do you think the locusts eat every leaf, ear, and stalk of the plants? _____
   _____

4. Do you think the locusts like corn? Why or why not? _____
   _____

**Vocabulary Fun:**

Color the picture that best matches the word.

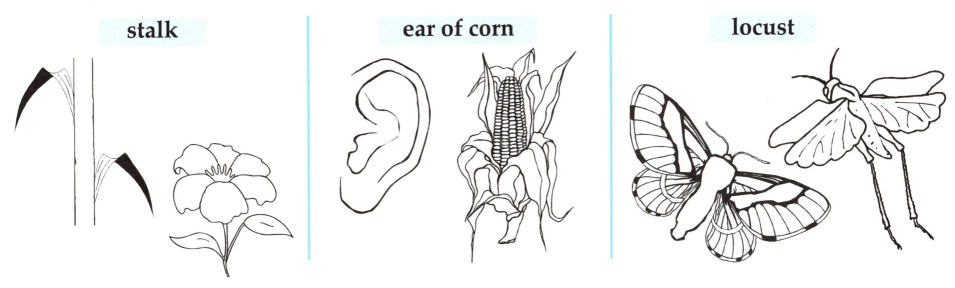

stalk        ear of corn        locust

# 19 Rubber Trees

Some farmers grow tall, gray rubber trees. They cut a groove in each trunk to get the white sap inside. The sap flows from the groove down a spout into a cup. The sap dries into a soft, sticky rubber.

**Multiple Sentence**
Date: _____

**Vocabulary to Visualize:**

**rubber tree:** tree that has sap inside that can be turned into rubber
**farmer:** man or woman who grow plants on a farm
**groove:** a long, skinny cut
**sap:** a liquid that carries water and food through a plant
**spout:** a tube or half a pipe used to guide the flow of liquid

## A  Picture This: Some farmers grow tall, gray rubber trees. They cut a groove in each trunk to get the white sap inside.

Underline or write in the answer that best matches your own picture.

| | | | | |
|---|---|---|---|---|
| 1. | What did those words make you picture? | farmers getting sap | farmers getting cones | |
| 2. | Where did you see them get the sap? | from trees | from bushes | from flowers |
| 3. | How did you see them get the sap? | they slashed into the trunk | they cut the tree down | |
| 4. | What did you see for the tree trunk? | the main stem of the tree | a part of tree that grows from its side | |
| 5. | What did you see the farmers use to cut the trunks? | a spoon | a knife | a pen |
| 6. | What color did you picture the trunks? | _____ | | |
| 7. | What size did you picture the trees? | as big as a building | as big as a child | |
| 8. | How did you picture the groove the farmers cut into the trunk? | long slits | small holes | |
| 9. | What did you picture in the groove? | black ooze | white sap | |

**B** **Picture This:** The sap flows from the groove down a spout into a cup. The sap dries into a soft, sticky rubber.

Underline or write in the answer that best matches your own picture.

| | | | |
|---|---|---|---|
| 1. | What did those words make you picture? | sap turning into rubber | sap flowing to the ground |
| 2. | Where did you picture the sap? | in a puddle    in a cup | on a plate |
| 3. | How did you see the sap going into the cup? | dripped down the tree and spout | sucked by a hose |
| 4. | What color did you picture the sap? | _____ | |
| 5. | How did you see it drip? | fast like a stream | slow drops |
| 6. | How did you picture the sap? | thin like water | thick like honey |
| 7. | How did you see the sap dry to rubber? | all the wetness left it | it stayed wet |

**Picture Summary:**

Number these pictures in order:

## Word Summary:
Fill in the blanks using the words listed below.

Some farmers _____ tall, gray rubber trees. They cut a groove in each thick trunk to free the white _____ inside the tree. The sap flows down a spout and into a _____ . The sap dries into a soft, sticky _____ .

**grow     sap     cup     rubber**

## Main Idea:
Connect these with a line.

| Farmers make rubber from tree sap. | a detail |
| Farmers make syrup from tree sap. | main idea |
| Farmers cut grooves into the tree trunk. | wrong |

## Spelling Practice:
Trace then cover the word.     Air-write then pencil write the word.

farmer

trunk

## Vocabulary Check:
Draw a line from the word to its meaning.

| cut | split open or sliced |
| sap | a tube used to guide the flow of liquid |
| spout | a liquid that runs through a plant |
| rubber | a long, skinny cut |
| groove | the stretchy stuff tires are made of |

**HOT Questions:**

1. Why do you think the farmers want the sap? _____

   _____

2. Why do you think there are cups at the bottom of the grooves? Why not at the tops of the grooves? _____

   _____

3. Why do you think farmers might want to catch the sap in a cup? Why not a tissue or a sponge? _____

   _____

4. Do you think these farmers plant a lot of rubber trees or just a few? Explain. _____

   _____

**Vocabulary Fun:**

Color the picture that best matches the word.

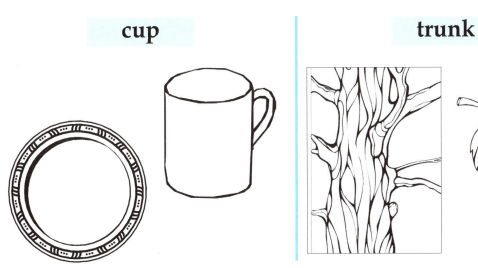

cup — trunk

farmer

# 20 Sun-Dried Grapes

Multiple Sentence
Date: _____

The men bend down all day to snip bunches of grapes from rows of green vines. Each ripe bunch is cut off at the stem and tossed in a basket. Full baskets are dumped on a big white sheet spread out on the ground. The grapes dry for days in the hot sun, and then get picked up as raisins.

**Vocabulary to Visualize:**

**grapes:** small round fruits that grow in bunch
**vine:** plant with long stems that can grow and wrap around fences or trees
**ripe:** ready to eat; fully grown
**bunch:** a group of things
**raisin:** dried grape

## A

**Picture This:** The men bend down all day to snip bunches of grapes from rows of green vines. Each ripe bunch is cut off at the stem and tossed in a basket.

Underline or write in the answer that best matches your own picture.

1. What did those words make you picture?  men getting grapes  men getting cherries
2. How did you see the men snipping the grapes from the vines?  cut with scissors  cut with spoons
3. What part of the grape vine did you see them snipping?  the fruit  the stems
4. What color did you picture the stems? _____
5. How did you see the men bending down?  legs straight, backs straight  legs bent, backs bent
6. How did you see them toss the grapes?  threw the bunches lightly  pitched the bunches with force
7. Where did you see them toss the grapes?  in a metal pan  onto the grass  in a woven basket
8. What color did you picture the grapes? _____

**Picture This:** Full baskets are dumped on a big white sheet spread out on the ground. The grapes dry for days in the hot sun, and then get picked up as raisins.

Underline or write in the answer that best matches your own picture.

1. What did those words make you picture?     grapes becoming raisins     grapes becoming juice
2. How did you see the men dump the grapes?     turned basket over     piled baskets on top of each other
3. Where did you see the men dump the grapes?     on the sheet     on the dirt
4. What color did you picture the sheet? _____
5. How did you see the sun?     covered by clouds     big, bright, and hot
6. What did you see for the texture of the grapes?     smooth     wrinkled     shiny
7. How did you see the grapes drying?     getting bigger and fatter     getting small and shriveled

**Picture Summary:**

Number these pictures in order:

**Word Summary:**
Fill in the blanks using the words listed below.

The men _____ bunches of grapes from rows of green vines. Each _____ was cut off at the stem and tossed in a basket. Full baskets were dumped on a big white _____ on the ground. The grapes _____ for days in the hot sun, and then got picked up as raisins.

**bunch     snipped     sheet     dried**

**Main Idea:**
Connect these with a line.

| Grapes are gathered and dried into raisins. | a detail |
| Grapes dry in the sun for days. | main idea |
| Raisins are gathered and dried into grapes. | wrong |

**Spelling Practice:**
Trace then cover the word.      Air-write then pencil write the word.

**Vocabulary Check:**
Draw a line from the word to its meaning.

| basket | a group of things |
| grapes | small round fruits |
| vine | a bowl woven from grasses |
| ripe | plant with a long stem that wraps |
| bunch | ready to eat |

**HOT Questions:**

1. Why do you think the grapes are dried on a sheet and not on the grass? _____

_____

2. Why do you think they put the grapes in baskets and not cups? _____

_____

3. Why do you think they spread the grapes out instead of piling them? _____

_____

4. How long do you think the grapes take to dry? _____

_____

**Vocabulary Fun:**

Color the picture that best matches the word.

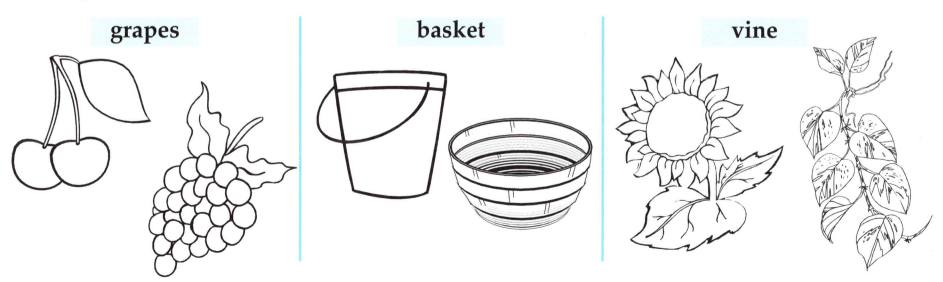

# Notes

**Analysis of Student Performance:**

# Notes

**Analysis of Student Performance:**

# Notes

**Analysis of Student Performance:**

___

## *Visualizing and Verbalizing® Graded Workbooks* Color Coding

The colored checkers along the book's spine represent the grade level of the workbook. For example, the two blue checkers indicate that the workbook is written at a second grade reading level. The colored star helps differentiate between books a, b, and c in each workbook set.